Homework Booklet

W9-BKE-529

I Love Reading

Level 6

by
Linda Denstaedt

Published by Instructional Fair
an imprint of
Frank Schaffer Publications®

Frank Schaffer Publications®

Send all inquiries to:
Frank Schaffer Publications
8720 Orion Place
Columbus, OH 43240

I Love Reading—grade 6

ISBN 1-56822-831-7

2 3 4 5 6 7 8 9 PAT 11 10 09 08 07

TABLE OF CONTENTS

The Sad Story of Seven Birds 2
From Slave to Inventor...4
Milk: Not for Everybody 6
Man's Super-Structure 8
Violent Crime Declining...10
Ancient Surgery 12
Early Writing Is Still Writing 14
Cross-Country or Downhill? 16
I Need My Eight Hours 18
Making Old-Fashioned Fudge 20
Icebiking: Challenge, Insanity, or Fun? 22
How Cold Is It Really?...24
Replaced but Not Forgotten 26
From Poor Farm Boy to President 28
Before Television, There Was Radio 30
From Dreams to Reality 32
Planning a Budget and Sticking to It 34
I Just Talk on It..36
Sending Love Through Cyberspace 38
The Lesson 40
By Saturday Noon 42
To the Moon 44
Can You Name the Seven Dwarfs? 46
One Afternoon in March...48
Trouble Is My Middle Name 50
Stephen's Secret 52
You Are a Winner 54
Free Kittens...56
How Can You Believe That? 58
It's Not My Fault!..60
Sleepwalking...62
Finding My Keys 64
Who Should Win?..66
How Could This Happen to Me? 68
Sollie, the Rock...70
I Never Thought of That...72
Answer Key 74

THE SAD STORY OF SEVEN BIRDS

If birds could talk, they might surprise you. Instead of describing the freedom of the skies, they might tell a sad story. They might talk about their struggles finding food, a place to live, and escaping mass destruction. It would sound more like the saga of a difficult life rather than the carefree existence you might imagine. In fact, if seven extinct birds told their sad stories, man would be the culprit in the destruction of all seven. *All the Birds of North America* by Jack L. Griggs states the sad history of these seven birds.

Hunters Destroy Bird Populations

Being easy prey to hunters was the cause of three birds' extinction. The great auk was lost by 1844. These birds were easily captured by fishermen and sailors who visited their nesting grounds in the North Atlantic. Sailors used them for food or bait. The passenger pigeon was abundant in the United States. Huge flocks darkened the skies. They nested and fed in flocks several miles wide. It was easy for commercial hunters to capture them in nets. They were sold to markets and restaurants. The last bird died in 1914. Likewise, the heath hen was a dining favorite and disappeared in 1932, even though hunting laws were changed to protect them in 1824.

Settlers Destroy Bird Populations

Being victim of disappearing nesting grounds and habitats was the major cause of extinction for the remaining four birds. The Labrador duck became extinct when settlers introduced dogs and cats to its habitat. It was also hunted, and it disappeared by 1875. The ivory-billed woodpecker was hunted for its decorative bill and feathers, but clearing the old forests for farming finally destroyed them in 1948. The Bachman's Warbler populations also disappeared gradually by 1949 when the forests were cleared. And finally, as settlers moved into southern states, the Carolina parakeet moved to remote areas in Florida until it was destroyed as a pest to fruit trees.

 1-56822-831-7

1. Circle two words in the title that help you determine the main idea.

   The Sad Story of Seven Birds

2. Circle two words in each subtitle that help determine the main idea.

   Hunters Destroy Bird Populations
   Settlers Destroy Bird Populations

3. Circle the words in the three topic sentences that help you determine the main idea.

   In fact, if seven extinct birds told their sad story, man would be the culprit in the destruction of all seven.

   Being prey to hunters was the cause of three birds' extinction.

   Being victim of disappearing nesting grounds and habitats was the major cause of extinction for the remaining four birds.

4. What is the main idea of this passage?
   A. Birds have sad lives.
   B. Seven birds are extinct today.
   C. Man caused the extinction of seven birds.

5. Circle the parts of the passage that were the most helpful in determining the main idea.
   Title   Subtitle   Topic Sentences

6. Write a more helpful title for this passage.

   _____

FROM SLAVE TO INVENTOR

George Washington Carver worked hard to become an inventor. Born a slave, he became famous and saved Southern farmers. He worked his way through high school and college. He received a degree from Iowa State Agricultural School and became a professor at Tuskegee University. He was an inventor and an expert in farming. In 1923 he received the Sprinam Medal for his accomplishments.

Carver is most famous for agricultural experiments with peanuts, sweet potatoes, and soybeans. As a professor at Tuskegee University, he experimented with various plants, searching for a crop that could grow in the overworked soil damaged by planting cotton. He discovered hundreds of uses for these plants. He invented over 300 uses for peanuts and over 100 uses for sweet potatoes.

A major reason he returned to the South was to help farmers. The soil had been damaged from planting cotton. Farmers were struggling. Carver taught both black and white farmers how to improve their soil. Through his research, he discovered that the peanut could grow in the damaged soil and could improve the soil as well. He turned the peanut into an important crop that aided farmers and improved the economy.

Carver's work changed farming and turned the peanut into a major cash crop. At first people did not believe his research. Previously the peanut was considered an unwanted plant. However, Carver ignored the ignorant reactions of people. He held seminars and traveled around the South educating farmers on planting, harvesting, plowing, and producing peanuts. As a result, the peanut became one of the major crops grown in the South.

1. Circle the words in the topic sentences that summarize the main idea of each paragraph.

   A. George Washington Carver worked hard to become an inventor.

   B. Carver is most famous for agricultural experiments with peanuts, sweet potatoes, and soybeans.

   C. A major reason he returned to the South was to help farmers.

   D. Carver's work changed farming and turned the peanut into a major cash crop.

2. What is the main idea of the passage?
   A. George Washington Carver was an inventor.
   B. George Washington Carver helped Southern farmers.
   C. George Washington Carver changed his life and changed the South.

3. What would be a better title for the passage?

   _____

4. Write a topic sentence for the paragraph below.

   He was offered jobs that paid more money than his position at Tuskegee University. He did not publish his research. He wanted to give his knowledge to the farmers and helped anyone who asked.

   _____

     5   1-56822-831-7

Milk: Not for Everybody

What would chocolate cake be without a big, cold glass of milk? What's the perfect companion to a peanut butter sandwich? A glass of milk is the answer. What goes best with eggs and toast? Milk, again. What would a ham sandwich be without a slice of cheese? As a matter of fact, many Americans could not imagine life without a glass of milk at every meal.

Some people say that milk is the perfect food. Milk contains calcium, vitamins A, C, and D. Babies live on it. Adults enjoy it. Ice cream and cheese come from milk. It seems that milk and milk products are a basic in everyone's life. However, many people cannot drink milk.

Milk may be a basic food for infants and small children, but adults can have difficulty digesting milk. People who cannot digest milk have lactose intolerance. This problem occurs in many adults. Drinking milk causes intestinal pain and gas. This problem occurs because some adults lack the enzyme to digest milk. Children have the enzyme lactase which breaks down the sugar lactose. However, as people age, they lose the ability to produce this enzyme, and milk becomes harder to digest.

Lactose intolerance is not a disease. It is caused by genes. People who live in certain areas of the world develop genes necessary for survival. It is believed that people who have lactose intolerance carry a gene that slows down as it ages. Children with this gene can produce lactase and digest milk easily. However, adults with this same gene will have difficulty as their bodies stop producing the lactase enzyme.

Getting the Main Idea

1. List three details you learned about milk.

2. List eight key vocabulary words necessary to understand lactose intolerance.

3. Explain lactose intolerance in your own words. Use the key vocabulary listed above. Do not look back at the passage.

4. Summarize the main idea of this article in a single sentence.

MAN'S SUPER-STRUCTURE

When you look at a bone on your dinner plate, you see a hard, white thing. You might imagine that your bones are also hard. However, bones are living organs. Like your heart or lungs, bones provide an important and necessary service to the body.

Bones are the super-structure of the human body. They support muscles and organs and give the body its size and shape. Bones grow as a person's body grows. They become thicker and stronger to do their job. Bones require nourishment just like other organs to remain strong.

Bones contain nerve tissue and blood vessels which continually feed this complex organ. Bones are continually being replaced, producing a hormone to reduce the damage done by the stress of daily living. Osteoclasts and osteoblasts are bone cells that continually work at rebuilding bones.

Bones are filled with connective tissue called *marrow*. Bone marrow also works for the body. Yellow bone marrow contains fat, but red bone marrow makes red and white blood cells and blood platelets. The body is in constant need of blood cells and blood platelets.

1. List three details you learned about bones.

   _____

   _____

   _____

2. List six key vocabulary words necessary to understand how bones function.

   _____

   _____

3. In your own words, explain how bones are organs. Use the key vocabulary listed above. Do not look back at the passage.

   _____

   _____

   _____

   _____

   _____

   _____

4. Summarize the main idea of this article in a single sentence.

   _____

   _____

VIOLENT CRIME DECLINING

Violent crime is declining, according to the U.S. Department of Justice. In 1996 the bureau reported 3,262,079 violent crimes. In 1973 violent crimes numbered 3,590,492. The Bureau of Justice Statistics publishes the rate of serious violent crime. The Justice Bureau collects information from two sources: crime and arrest reports and a household survey completed twice a year. The National Crime Victimization Survey interviews people 12 and above from 45,000 homes. The total number of people surveyed each year is about 94,000.

The four measures used by the Bureau to determine the rate of serious violent crime are as follows:
1. The number of homicides, rapes, robberies, and aggravated assaults recorded by police and reported by a survey, even if they were not reported to the police.
2. The number of homicides, rapes, robberies, and aggravated assaults individuals taking the survey said were reported to the police.
3. The number of homicides, rapes, robberies, and aggravated assaults in the Uniform Crime Report of the FBI. This information does not include commercial robberies or victims under age 12.
4. The number of homicides, rapes, robberies, and aggravated assaults recorded by police and reported to the FBI. The graph below indicates their findings from 1973 to the present.

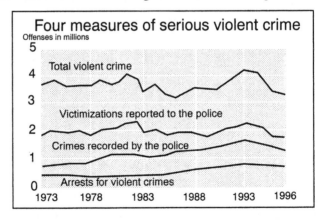

Four measures of serious violent crime

Bureau of Justice Statistics. Crime Trends, 1997: Executive Summary. Washington, D.C.: U.S. Department of Justice

1. List the serious violent crimes monitored by the U.S. Justice Department.

   _____

2. List the two methods the U.S. Justice Department uses to gather information on crime.

   _____   _____

3. List four measures the U.S. Justice Department uses to determine the crime rate.

   _____   _____

   _____   _____

4. How much has Total Violent Crime decreased from 1973 to 1996?

   _____

5. Have arrests for violent crimes increased or decreased since 1973?

   _____

6. Review the graph. Review the methods the Justice Department uses to gather information. Can you trust the information provided? Has serious violent crime really declined? Circle one: Yes No. Explain your answer.

   _____

   _____

   _____

ANCIENT SURGERY

Archaeologists discovered a 5,000-year-old skull of a man in France. The skull had two holes with small pieces of bone removed. One hole was about two inches wide. The other hole was about three inches wide. However, there was no indication the man died a violent death. In fact, there is clear evidence that the holes were caused by ancient surgery.

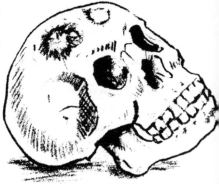

Amelie A. Walker reported in *Archaeology* that researchers speculate the holes were caused by a surgical procedure called *trepanation*. Trepanation is the oldest surgical technique known to archaeologists. Trepanation is an operation in which a small piece of bone is removed from the skull. Holes are drilled into the skull and a section of bone is removed. Why ancient people used trepanation is not understood. Trepanation is still used in Africa today. Therefore, researchers imagine ancients used the operation for similar reasons. It is believed they used it to cure pressure on the brain, or, possibly, the patient had headaches, epilepsy, or was mentally ill.

The holes in the newly discovered skull appear to have been made by a sharp object, possibly flint. Flint was extremely sharp and could easily have made the cuts. The holes were carefully scraped and cut into the skull. The procedure must have been successful since the skull had already begun to grow back. There was no indication the man died from infection, so researchers imagine the operation was not the cause of the man's death.

This discovery made by archaeologists at Freiburg University provides solid proof that man used surgical procedures effectively probably farther back than 5,000 years ago. Scientists believe that a surgery this delicate must have been used for many years to be so effective and not kill the patient.

1. Archaeologists are like detectives. They find things buried for thousands of years and study the objects to understand life during that time. List three facts that are clear evidence the holes in the 5,000-year-old skull were caused by surgery.

_____

_____

_____

2. List four possible reasons a person would have trepanation.

_____

_____

3. What information did archaeologists use to come to this conclusion?

_____

_____

_____

4. What information did archaeologists use to come to the conclusion that ancient surgery probably occurred farther back than 5,000 years?

_____

_____

EARLY WRITING IS STILL WRITING

Remember when you were just four or five years old, and you pulled out your crayons and wrote Grandma a letter? You drew circles and lines. Some may even have been connected. You may have created a loopy script that looked more like art than writing. When you gave the note to Grandma, she let you read it aloud. It may have seemed like a game, but the truth is that you were really writing.

Years ago people believed that children could not write until they could spell. Children practiced letters or were given spelling words or dictation to copy, but schools did not consider scribbling to be writing. Children in early elementary school spent their time painting or playing with blocks or clay. Scribbling then was just scribbling.

However, now teachers believe that encouraging young children to scribble is really an important step in writing. This early writing may not be readable, but it is still writing. This early writing does not even have to look like writing, yet it is still writing. Teachers have discovered that it is important for children to write before they even know their alphabet. Young children should be allowed to write lists and tell stories, leave messages and make signs. They should be asked to read their writing aloud even if it is unreadable.

This may seem like a game of pretend, but it is really a step toward real writing. If children are told they cannot write until they can spell the words, their ability to read and write later in life will be reduced. Teachers are discovering that children who are engaged in early writing before five years old are better readers.

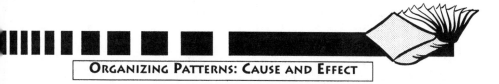

1. Use the two-column note-taking system to draw conclusions about early writing.

Misconceptions About Early Writing	
Discoveries About Early Writing	

2. What happens to children who are expected to write before they know their alphabet?

_____

_____

3. Do you agree with current thinking on writing instruction? Circle one: Yes   No   Explain your answer.

_____

_____

_____

_____

CROSS-COUNTRY OR DOWNHILL?

The answer to this question makes a big difference if you are a skier. Both forms of skiing are popular and can be done by people of all ages. Both require snow, and both can be done for relaxation or competition. So what makes the two methods of skiing so different?

Cross-country skiing means just that—you ski across the country. You do not need tall hills or ski lifts to ski cross-country. You simply need snow and equipment. Cross-country skiers can go skiing right outside their back door. Even land that is flat can be enjoyable for the cross-country skier. Cross-country races can be 50 minutes long or two hours long. These long races require strength and endurance. Races vary in length from 9 miles to 30 miles.

Downhill skiing also is named for the activity. A downhill skier skis down hills. That means the skier needs tall hills and a means to get up to the top. Downhill skiing takes place at ski resorts. Downhill races are short. The goal is to get down the hill the fastest without falling. Speed is the goal, and downhill racers can go faster than 80 miles per hour.

Both types of skiing require special equipment. However, downhill skis are wider and shorter than cross-country skis. The boots are also different. Downhill boots are larger and protect the ankles from injury. They are connected to the ski at the heel and toe with a binding. Cross-country boots are like shoes, flexible and usually fit below the ankle. They are attached to the ski at the toe only. Both types of skiing require ski poles; however, the poles are used for different purposes. A downhill skier uses poles for balance and direction. A cross-country skier uses poles as part of the glide-step technique.

 1-56822-831-7

1. Complete the Venn diagram below listing the similarities and differences between cross-country and downhill skiing.

Cross-country skiing   Downhill skiing

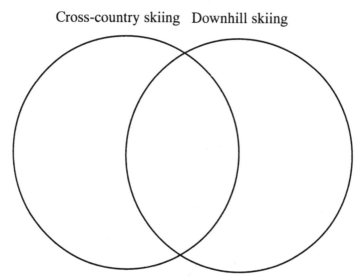

2. Which type of skiing is the easiest to do? _____
   Explain your answer. Use facts from the diagram to support your opinion.

   _____

   _____

3. Which type of skiing is the most expensive to do? _____
   Explain your answer. Use facts from the diagram to support your opinion.

   _____

   _____

1-56822-831-7

I Need My Eight Hours

Many people cannot function if they do not have eight hours of sleep every night. Other people can function just fine on six hours or less. How much sleep do you need?

Babies need at least 16 hours of sleep, but as they grow, their need for sleep diminishes. By the time children reach the teen years, they have flipped their sleeping and waking time and require only about eight hours of sleep a night.

Sleep researchers have discovered four stages of sleep from light sleep to deep sleep. A person moves through the stages toward deep or REM sleep. Dreaming occurs during REM sleep about an hour or so after a person falls asleep. Dreaming occurs several times during the night as the sleep cycle is repeated every hour and a half or so.

People who cannot go to sleep have a problem called *insomnia*. This is a common problem which can be caused by physical problems or just too much caffeine. People who have difficulty staying awake and fall asleep easily during the day have a problem called *narcolepsy*. This is a genetic problem which can cause a person to fall asleep several times during the day. People who have frequent nightmares or sleep walk have a problem called *somnambulism*. This problem usually disappears in adulthood.

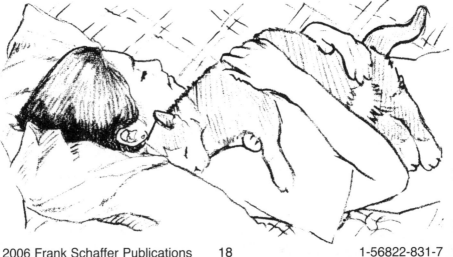

1. How many stages of sleep are there? _____

2. How long is a single sleep cycle? _____

3. When does dreaming occur? _____

4. How much sleep does the average young adult need? _____

5. How much sleep does the average *infant* need? _____

6. How many hours did you sleep last night? _____

7. Did you get enough sleep? _____

8. Using the facts from the passage, create a graph that illustrates the number of sleep cycles you achieved last night.

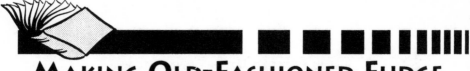

Making Old-Fashioned Fudge

Making fudge the old-fashioned way is not easy. It requires patience and skill, but it can be worth all the effort. Perfect fudge has a smooth consistency that is creamy and tastes like what you buy in the fudge shops you visit while on vacation.

If you like old-fashioned fudge, you will want to make it the old-fashioned way. This requires patience and a few important tools. First, you need a large, heavy sauce pan, a candy thermometer, and a wooden spoon. You also want to have a larger saucepan filled with water ready to cool the candy quickly and stop the cooking process.

Second, you need patience. You will combine sugar, heavy milk, and powdered cocoa and stand next to the stove, slowly stirring until the mixture boils. You will have to watch it closely.

Third, once the sugar crystals begin to slip easily down the side of the pan, you will stop stirring and watch the boiling sugar until it reaches the soft-ball stage. This is easy to determine if you have a candy thermometer. However, if you do not, you have to guess by dropping the mixture into a glass of cold water. When the mixture forms a small ball, it is ready. Finally, you must quickly remove the mixture from the heat, add butter and vanilla, and beat the fudge into a glossy sheen.

If you do not have these basic tools or the patience, you might consider doing it the new, foolproof method. Most modern fudge recipes are made with chocolate chips or marshmallow cream. They allow you to use a microwave oven, which reduces the need to stand on guard at the stove. Plus, the microwave does most of the work—no stirring, no pots and mess, no beating to a glossy sheen. These recipes create foolproof fudge that tastes almost as good as the old-fashioned kind.

 1-56822-831-7

1. List two advantages of making fudge the old-fashioned way.

   _____

   _____

2. List two disadvantages of making fudge the old-fashioned way.

   _____

   _____

3. List the steps in making old-fashioned fudge.

   _____

   _____

   _____

   _____

4. Why is the modern method of making fudge easier?

   _____

5. What steps in making old-fashioned fudge would be deleted with the modern method?

   _____

   _____

   _____

Icebiking: Challenge, Insanity, or Fun?

Imagine this. It is -10° outside. A fresh layer of glistening snow covers the ground. You hop out of bed, eat breakfast, pull on the cold weather gear, and hop on your bike. For some people this thought is unimaginable. Riding a bike anywhere in winter seems crazy.

However, there are hardy individuals who believe icebiking is not insanity. For them, it is an enjoyable form of recreation or even a way to commute to work. Icebikers race, go on camping trips, and continue the activities many of us reserve for summertime.

If you think icebiking sounds like fun to you, it is easy to get started. Icebikers suggest that starting is as easy as not putting your bike away when the weather gets cold. Just continue riding your bike. Icebikers suggest that you might not make it through the first winter. Just ride your bike one day at a time. Plus, don't be foolhardy. Pay attention to the wind chill and do not bike when it gets to -40°.

As the weather gets colder, you have to dress appropriately, but do not overdress. Biking produces a lot of heat. Two areas that require special attention are hands and feet. Bikers will need warm gloves and boots that protect against wet and cold and should always wear a helmet.

You may need to change your tires when the snow begins. Trade in those summer tires for studded tires which provide better traction. You will have to learn how to ride on snow and ice. The payoff is big: you enjoy nature, get great exercise, and do a little bit to reduce pollution.

If you are really serious, you may need additional advice. Icebikers can access a Web site for history or participate in a photography contest. The Web address is http://www.enteract.com/~icebike/ and "Icebiker," the Web master, gives excellent advice on equipment and clothing.

1. List two reasons you enjoy riding your bike.

   _____

   _____

2. List two reasons icebikers enjoy riding bikes.

   _____

   _____

3. What keeps most people from enjoying biking year round?

   _____

4. How can you get started icebiking?

   _____

5. What special equipment or clothing is required to icebike?

   _____

   _____

6. Answer the question the title poses. Is icebiking a challenge, insanity, or fun?

   _____

How Cold Is It Really?

If you enjoy winter sports, you keep a close eye on the temperature. When the thermometer reaches 32°F, water freezes. However, 32°F is also the perfect temperature for many winter sports. Skiers, sliders, and skaters look forward to days when the temperatures dip below freezing. To them, freezing temperatures are not freezing at all.

However, the thermometer alone does not determine how cold it is outside. The thermometer will register only the temperature of the air. Any sports enthusiast knows to pay close attention to the wind as well. Wind chill can make a 32°F day feel much colder.

What is wind chill? When you add the wind speed and the temperature together, you get the wind chill. This can be a dangerous combination. A 20-mile-per-hour wind can turn a 25°F day into -3°F. As a result, skin exposed to extremely cold temperatures can freeze. Frostbite, which usually occurs at 10°F, can occur at 32°F if other weather conditions such as wind are present.

Use the wind chill chart developed in 1941 by Siple and Passel to help you determine how to dress for winter sports.

Table of Windchill Values: English Units

Windspeed (mph)	Air Temperature (degrees F)															
	45	40	35	30	25	20	15	10	5	0	-5	-10	-15	-20	-25	-30
5	43	37	32	27	22	16	11	6	0	-5	-10	-15	-21	-26	-31	-36
10	34	28	22	16	10	3	-3	-9	-15	-21	-27	-34	-40	-46	-52	-58
15	29	22	15	9	2	-5	-12	-18	-25	-32	-38	-45	-52	-59	-65	-72
20	25	18	11	4	-3	-11	-18	-25	-32	-39	-46	-53	-60	-68	-75	-82
25	22	15	8	0	-7	-15	-22	-30	-37	-44	-52	-59	-67	-74	-82	-89
30	20	13	5	-3	-10	-18	-25	-33	-41	-48	-56	-64	-71	-79	-87	-94
35	19	11	3	-5	-12	-20	-28	-36	-44	-51	-59	-67	-75	-83	-90	-98
40	18	10	2	-6	-14	-22	-30	-38	-46	-53	-61	-69	-77	-85	-93	-101
45	17	9	1	-7	-15	-23	-31	-39	-47	-55	-63	-71	-79	-87	-95	-103
50	17	9	1	-7	-15	-23	-31	-40	-48	-56	-64	-72	-80	-88	-96	-104

Source: NCAR Atmospheric Technology Division

 1-56822-831-7

1. At what temperature does water freeze?_____

2. At what temperature does frostbite occur? _____

3. What factors can make frostbite occur at 32°F?_____

4. Use the wind chill chart to determine how cold it really is outside.

    A. A sunny day of 20°F, but the wind is blowing at 15 mph.____

    B. A cloudy day of 0°F, but the wind is blowing at 5 mph. ____

    C. A sunny day of 15°F, but the wind is blowing at 10 mph.____

    D. A cloudy day of -5°F, but the wind is blowing at 4 mph. ____

5. Which of the following weather conditions are helpful indicators
    of frostbite danger?

    _____ A. Sun and temperature

    _____ B. Sun, temperature, and wind

    _____ C. Clouds and wind

    _____ D. Temperature and wind

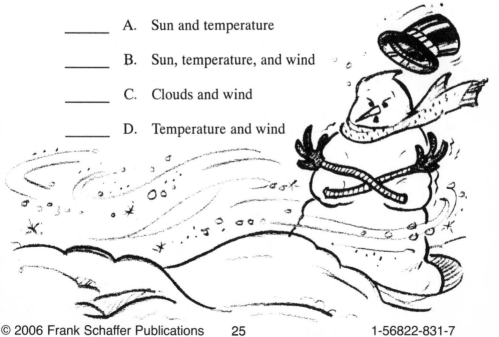

REPLACED BUT NOT FORGOTTEN

Lighthouses were and still are important to navigation on oceans and large lakes. Early lighthouses were simply fires used to warn travelers of rocks, shallow water, or other dangers. Lighthouses warned against these dangers day and night. They became especially important during the night, fog, or bad weather. Ship captains used charts to set a course, but the lighthouses aided a ship off course or in unfamiliar waters.

Eventually, structures were built and manned by people called *lighthouse keepers*. These individuals lived in a small home attached to the lighthouse and kept the light blazing. They also maintained the lighthouse. Often they were called upon to save people who came too close to the rocky shores the lighthouses warned against.

Today, lighthouses still exist, but they use the same type of lights used at airports. These large electric lights can be seen on the old lighthouses, light ships, and buoys. The U.S. Coast Guard maintains the lighthouses in and around the United States.

Although lighthouses still serve an important service, navigation has improved, and many ships use radar to help them navigate and avoid dangerous waters. As a result, lighthouse keepers rarely are called upon to save people who have run aground or are lost in a storm.

1. Complete the Venn diagram below, listing the similarities and differences between historic lighthouses and lighthouses today.

Historic Lighthouses   Lighthouses of Today

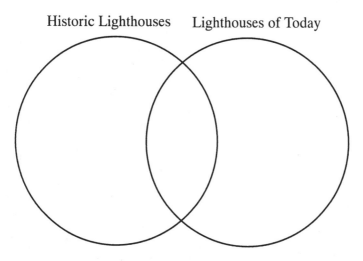

2. Why would boats and ship captains still need lighthouses today? Explain your answer. Use facts from the Venn diagram to support your opinion.

_____

_____

3. Why would lighthouse keepers today rarely have to rescue people? Explain your answer. Use facts from the diagram to support your opinion.

_____

_____

From Poor Farm Boy to President

Abraham Lincoln was a poor farm boy, a lawyer, and a congressman. In 1860 he was elected sixteenth president of the United States.

He was a dedicated statesman. He valued human rights and opposed slavery. He worked to restrict it.

Whoever first said that anyone could be president was probably thinking of Abraham Lincoln. As a child, Lincoln was highly motivated to learn. He had little formal education but educated himself reading books by firelight. He believed anyone who gave him a book was a good friend, since books held the power of knowledge.

Lincoln was always known for his honesty. Before studying law, he was a shopkeeper. But his partner died, and his shop failed. He was also a postmaster, clerked at a store, and split rails for a living before he turned to law and politics.

As president, Lincoln may be best known for freeing the slaves, but he was a master statesman and a wise commander-in-chief. His election contributed to the secession of six Southern states and eventually the Civil War. He was also an excellent speaker who wrote his speeches himself. His most famous speech is the Gettysburg Address. Lincoln was assassinated by John Wilkes Booth, an actor. Booth shot Lincoln from behind in Ford's Theatre in Washington, D.C., and Lincoln died the next day.

1. List six jobs Lincoln had before becoming president.

   _____ _____ _____

   _____ _____ _____

2. List three words that describe Lincoln.

   _____ _____ _____

3. Is the passage written in chronological order? Circle one: Yes   No

4. What words in each paragraph indicate time?

   Paragraph #1 _____

   Paragraph #2 _____

   Paragraph #3 _____

   Paragraph #4 _____

   Paragraph #5 _____

5. Insert the paragraphs on the time line below. Use the words that
   indicate time to determine where a paragraph belongs on the time
   line.

   ├──┼────┼
   Born: 1809   Elected President: 1860 Died: 1865

   Paragraph #__ Paragraph #__ Paragraph #__ Paragraph #__ Paragraph #__

BEFORE TELEVISION, THERE WAS RADIO

What did people do for entertainment before television? Today the average child spends more time watching television than reading. Television is so much a part of daily life, many people cannot imagine what life was like before it.

Before television, there was radio. Radio was invented around 1916 from the telegraph. At first, it was used to get information quickly from one part of the country to another. By 1926 radios were common in homes. People listened to music, news, and special shows in the same way we watch television today. Television was not invented until the 1940s, and it did not gain popularity in homes until 1955.

Families would gather around their radios and listen to shows broadcast all over the world. One of the most popular radio shows was "The Lone Ranger." The show was about a Texas Ranger and a faithful Indian, named Tonto, who tirelessly worked to stop evil. The Lone Ranger rode a white horse named Silver and wore a black mask. He hid his identity because he had been left for dead by a gang that ambushed and killed five other Texas Rangers. He vowed to find these desperadoes. His famous yell, "Hi-O Silver," his white hat, white horse, and black mask became symbols of the American Wild West hero.

Other famous radio heroes were The Shadow and The Green Hornet. Eventually, radio shows became famous television shows as well. Comedians and vaudeville stars made the transition from the stage to radio and finally television too. Comedians like Jack Benny, Red Skelton, and George Burns had radio shows that became television favorites.

         1-56822-831-7

1. List three heroes who got their start on radio.

   _____ _____ _____

2. List three comedians who got their start on radio.

   _____ _____ _____

3. List three ways radio and television are alike.

   _____ _____ _____

4. Which form of entertainment became popular in homes more quickly? Circle one: Radio Television   Support your answer with facts from the passage.

   _____

   _____

   _____

5. List three facts about the Lone Ranger.

   _____

   _____

   _____

   _____

   _____

   _____

FROM DREAMS TO REALITY

Man has probably always dreamed of flight. As he watched birds fly, he wished he, too, could soar into the blue, blue sky. As he watched the night sky, he wished he could explore the distant bright specks called stars. These dreams led inventors and scientists to risk their lives to achieve flight.

Orville and Wilbur Wright's first flight at Kitty Hawk in 1903 was only the beginning. When man achieved the skies, he did not stop until he achieved the stars. The first manned space flight occurred in 1961 when Russian cosmonaut, Yuri A. Gagarin, orbited earth a single time. In 1963 the first woman cosmonaut, Valentina Tereshkova, orbited earth 48 times.

The Russians led the race to space for many years. In 1965 another cosmonaut, Alesksei A. Leonov took the first space walk. In 1968 the Russians launched an unmanned spacecraft that orbited the moon. The pictures that returned to earth encouraged man to take the next step: land on the moon.

The United States became the leader in the space race when *Apollo 11* landed on the moon in 1969. Neil Armstrong was the first man to step on the lunar surface and said these famous words, "That's one small step for a man, one giant leap for mankind." Later in 1969 Charles Conrad, Jr., and Alan L. Bean returned to the moon for more exploration. In 1972 astronauts Young, Duke, and Mattingly took the last flight to the moon.

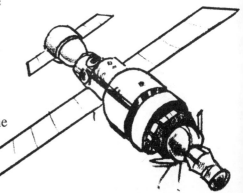

Today man continues his quest for space, gathering data from the *Mir* Space Station which was launched in 1986. In addition, unmanned probes have flown deep into space toward the planets, sending back pictures and scientific readings.

1. List six people who were important in man's quest for space.

   _____   _____   _____

   _____   _____   _____

2. Is this passage written in chronological order? Circle one: Yes No
   List the dates in the order they are used in the passage.

   ____ ____ ____ ____ ____ ____ ____ ____ ____

3. Fill in the table below. Insert the events in chronological order.

Manned Flights	Unmanned Flights

   1-56822-831-7

Planning a Budget and Sticking to It

Always running out of money? Ever wonder where your money goes? Saving for a special trip, activity, or object? If you answered yes to these three questions, it is time to plan a budget and stick to it.

The first step in building a livable budget is to record your spending habits. Look at your expenditures. Do you buy your lunch? Do you buy a soft drink or even water from a machine? You may discover you spend money foolishly. Buying a candy bar for $.50 every day may seem insignificant, but by the end of the month, it adds up to $15.00. Instead, put a snack in your backpack.

The next step is determining your debits and credits. Look at what comes in and what goes out. If you have determined your spending habits, you know what your debits are. Credits might be harder to determine if you do not have a job. Determine all the ways you get money. For example, count the dollars you earn or money given to you as presents. How much each week do you have available to spend? What are your sources of income? If you do not have a regular source of income, you need to find ways to make money. Do you have an allowance? Can you negotiate with your parents to raise your allowance? Offer to do more chores or special jobs that will increase your income. Check out the neighborhood. Lawn work and baby-sitting are two jobs for teenagers. Remember, your debits should not be more than your credits.

The last step is determining your cash flow and savings goals. How much money do you have available each week to spend? You might budget a small cash flow for yourself because you want to save for a new pair of skis, which means you might earn $10.00 a week, but only allow yourself to spend $3.00. Look at three important categories. How much money do you wish to save? How much money do you need for essentials? How much money do you want for frivolous activities? Determining the balance between savings goals and cash flow is an important decision for any budget.

1. Define the following terms. Then write the sentence or phrase that helped you determine its definition.

   expenditures _____

   debit _____

   credit _____

   cash flow _____

2. List the three steps in preparing a budget.

   1. _____

   2. _____

   3. _____

3. Describe your current approach to a budget. Use all the vocabulary from question #1 in your response.

   _____

   _____

   _____

   _____

   _____

I JUST TALK ON IT

The telephone is probably so much a part of your life, you do not even wonder how it works. It rings, you pick it up, you talk on it. If you access the Internet, you even use the telephone every day while working on your computer. The telephone is an important tool for daily life.

Telephones are big business. Millions of phones are in homes and businesses. Now cellular phones make phone conversations possible in cars, on planes and boats, or just walking down the street. There are even phones that project a picture of the caller, allowing people to have visual conversations.

So how does the telephone work? Your voice is transformed into a digital signal. Millions of these signals travel at an amazing speed on cables or fibers. Today, many phone conversations are carried over coaxial cables made of copper tubing. However, optical fibers are replacing these cables. Optical fibers are thin fibers which carry digitally coded light impulses. Phone conversations from the other side of the world use satellites. A conversation is sent from an antenna on earth to the satellite which relays it to another antenna.

The newest telephone craze is cellular phones. They provide convenience and ease. A person can make a call without being connected to either a coaxial cable or optical fiber system. These phones use radio transmissions to connect callers.

 1-56822-831-7

1. Circle the words in the sentences below that give a clue to the meaning of the italicized word.

   A. There are even phones that project a picture of the caller, allowing people to have *visual* conversations.

   B. A conversation is sent from an antenna on earth to the satellite which *relays* it to another antenna.

2. List four methods by which phone conversations are transmitted.

   _____

   _____

3. Describe how your phone conversations are probably transmitted. Indicate what type of phone equipment you use in your explanation. Use vocabulary from the reading.

   _____

   _____

   _____

   _____

   _____

   _____

Sending Love Through Cyberspace

Alex sat next to the girl of his dreams every day in science, math, and computer applications. Every day Sese smiled her pretty smile filled with silver wires just like Alex. She wrote notes to him during class, and she even laughed at his jokes. Alex thought that she liked him too. Unfortunately, he was too timid to speak, and he worried the year would pass without ever finding out for certain.

When Valentines Day arrived, Alex thought this was his chance. He could send her a special valentine to ensure Sese got the message that he really liked her. Unfortunately, Alex had no money. He couldn't afford flowers or candy. He didn't even have enough money to buy a fancy card. He was desperate—so desperate that he broke down and talked to his dad.

When Alex's dad said, "Try cyberspace," Alex was confused. He wondered how the Internet could help him. But when he visited the Free Virtual Valentine Web site, he knew this was the perfect place for him. He chose a musical valentine and e-mailed it to Sese at school.

On Valentine's Day, Alex waited impatiently for Sese to open her e-mail. He tried to look busy, but he watched her out of the corner of his eye. Sese whispered, "You sent me a message," as she clicked on the hot link to Alex's valentine.

"Yeah," Alex responded and leaned back in his chair. Then, music sang from Sese's computer. She smiled and blushed as she read the message. Then she turned to Alex and said, "You're great."

I'm great, he repeated to himself. She likes me, Alex thought. If only I'd found cyberspace a long time ago.

 1-56822-831-7

1. Circle two important words in the title that help predict the story's purpose.

   Sending Love in Cyberspace

2. What does *cyberspace* mean? _____

3. Circle the words below that help you to understand cyberspace.

math	science	computer applications
musical	valentine	flowers
Internet	Web site	e-mail

4. How did Alex use cyberspace to solve his problem?

   _____

   _____

5. What is the purpose of this story? _____

   A. To illustrate how to combat shyness with girls.
   B. To explain how Alex discovered if Sese liked him.
   C. To illustrate how to send a valentine through cyberspace.

6. What details in the story suggest Sese liked Alex even before he sent her the valentine?

   _____

   _____

THE LESSON

I'm not defending what I did. It was wrong, but spelling is hard. I tell myself, if I study harder, I'd do better, but I never do better. Plus, it's not the hard words that I miss. I can spell *conquistador, desegregation, geothermal,* or even *metamorphosis.* I just can't spell *heard, early,* or *cough.*

It's doubt. I doubt my abilities. At home, I resay Mrs. Wilson's advice: *"Heard" is easily confused with "herd." So remember that "heard," meaning to hear something, has an "ear" in it.* But I get to class, and Mrs. Wilson says, "Heard. I heard the band playing loudly. Heard." And I only remember it's a hard word that people confuse.

That's where I get into trouble. I start thinking about people. You see, I'm the "people" in that sentence that always get confused. I don't want to get confused, and so I start thinking: *Leah, you're gonna get this right. This word should have an "ear" in it, but it doesn't which is why kids get confused.* So I write down "herd." Of course, I get it wrong. Mrs. Wilson says: *These are the most frequently misspelled words. Lots of people have trouble with them.*

After the last "C," which got me grounded for a week, I devised the plan. I'd write the words on the palm of my hand, real small, so nobody would notice. I figured I could just flip my hand over and no more confusion. To be honest, I had a premonition things would go badly when I missed the bus and was late for school. I should have washed my hand off right then, but I didn't.

By sixth hour, the ink had smudged, and I couldn't read the words. Worse, Mrs. Wilson caught me looking at my hand. I got an "F" and got grounded for a month. However, not being able to do anything had an unexpected side benefit. I had lots of time to study spelling. I guess I'm not meant to be a cheater.

40 1-56822-831-7

1. What is the name of the narrator? _____

2. Why does she begin her story with the sentence, "I'm not defending what I did"?

   _____

   _____

3. Why did she decide to cheat?

   _____

   _____

4. What caused her to doubt her plan?

   _____

   _____

5. What lesson does she learn? Check all that apply.
   _____A. Do not cheat.
   _____B. Do not write the answers on your hand.
   _____C. Do not miss the bus.
   _____D. Do not be late for school.

      1-56822-831-7

By Saturday Noon

Saturday noon was one of those special times in our house. When I say special I don't mean good, special. You see, by Saturday noon, my sisters and I had to have our bedrooms totally clean.

Dad acted like an army sergeant doing the white-glove test. If anything was out of place, if any clothes were left on the floor, if your dresser wasn't cleaned off and shiny, you didn't get to go anywhere.

That wasn't hard for Margaret. She was a neat-freak, but Chelsea and I were normal, which was the problem—two normal sisters sharing one bedroom. On Monday we started our separate piles. You know, dirty clothes, wrinkled clothes, clothes that didn't look good on but you didn't want to hang up again. By Wednesday it was hard to find the floor. By Friday the dressers were loaded. Plus, Mom wouldn't let us throw everything down the laundry chute. "Sort it," she'd say. It took hours.

Usually, we had enough time to get it all folded and hung up by noon, but last Saturday, Chelsea got sick. She spent the morning vomiting, and I was left to clean the room, alone. I had plans to go shopping with Jen.

At 10: 00 Jen decided to leave early. I got desperate, shoved everything under Chelsea's bed, dusted the dressers, plumped the pillows, and called Dad for a room check.

He started the checklist, "Shiny dresser, nicely made bed, clean carpets," but stopped when he got to "empty closet." He turned and asked, "Sarah, where are all your clothes?"

"Dirty."

"Dirty?" he looked behind the dresser, then under the bed. "Dirty?"

I winced. "Oh, I must have missed those."

"Call Jen. You're not going shopping today," he said.

By Saturday noon, I was vomiting alongside Chelsea. Mom said, "Lucky you didn't go shopping." I figured it just the opposite. If I had gone shopping, I would never have gotten sick.

1. "Saturday Noon" is the title and is used three times in the story. Why is that time important to Sarah?

   _____

   _____

2. How is Margaret different from Sarah and Chelsea?

   _____

   _____

3. Sarah does not see her problem. She blames it on everyone else. State the problems she thinks others cause.

   Margaret _____

   Mother _____

   Chelsea _____

   Jen _____

4. Sarah says she is normal. Is Sarah normal? Circle one: Yes   No Explain your answer.

   _____

   _____

   _____

To the Moon

"Strike three. You're out!" shouted the umpire.

Adam dropped his shoulders as he walked back to the bench dragging the bat. He tossed the bat into the pile, flipped off the batting helmet, and sat on the bench.

"Hey, get it next time," Coach said, clapping his hands as Billy approached the plate. "Wait for your ball, Bill. We need this."

Adam pulled his hat down over his eyes, leaned against the chain-link fence, and folded his arms across his chest.

"To the moon," Steve elbowed Adam.

"Not funny. Three ups—three outs."

"Stop swinging like you're hitting a home run." Steve readjusted his hat.

Adam slumped then said, "Next time I'm bunting."

"Sure you will. When have you or I ever bunted in our lives?"

"Astronauts, man. We're astronauts." Adam leaped to his feet clapping as Billy's hit dropped just over the second-baseman's head.

"We got something goin'." Coach put his hand around Steve's shoulder. "Steve, nothin' fancy. Just a good hit. Get on base."

Steve adjusted his helmet, took two home-run swings, and rocked his feet into place.

"Strike one!" the umpire shouted.

Steve readjusted his helmet, knocked the bat against the plate, swung the bat into position, and rocked his feet into place.

"Strike two!" the umpire shouted.

Steve readjusted his helmet, took two practice swings, knocked the bat against the plate, rocked his feet into place, and pointed to the outfield. The outfielders backed up, the pitcher hesitated, then threw the pitch. Steve watched it gliding toward him, sweet as a slice of watermelon. At the last minute, he stepped out of his home-run stance, slid his hand up the bat and bunted.

"To the moon." Adam leaped into the air clapping. "To the moon."

         1-56822-831-7

1. "To the Moon" is the title and is used three times in the story. What does the phrase mean?

   _____

   _____

2. How are Steve and Adam alike?

   _____

   _____

3. Why does Adam think they are astronauts?

   _____

   _____

4. What details suggest that Steve also has a problem with striking out?

   _____

   _____

   _____

5. What caused Steve to bunt? Circle one.

   A. Steve was pitched a bad ball.
   B. Steve was told to bunt by the coach.
   C. Steve always bunted when he was frightened.
   D. Steve wanted to help the team win.

1-56822-831-7

Can You Name the Seven Dwarfs?

"What you wanna play?" Will shoved a bite of pancake into his mouth.

"Scrabble. We are Scrabble maniacs at this house," said Scott.

"How about," Will poured more orange juice, "what's that game you ask questions about dumb things everyone always forgets?"

"Trivial Pursuit," said Scott.

"Yeah, Trivial Pursuit."

"Can you name the seven dwarfs?" asked Eric.

"Snoopy, Sneezy, Dopey," said Scott.

"Snoopy is a dog. It's Sneezy, Dopey, Grumpy, Happy, Sleepy, and . . . ." Eric said.

"And," said Will.

"Doc," the boys said in unison.

"Yeah, I hate those games." Scott cut his pancake in half.

"Wait, that's only six dwarfs." Eric gulped his orange juice. "We're missing one. Sneezy, Dopey, Grumpy, Happy, Sleepy, Doc, and . . . and who?"

"Somebody," Will exaggerated the "e" at the end of *somebody*.

"Forget Trivial Pursuit. Let's play Scrabble," said Scott.

"Scrabble's too much like school. Let's play football," said Will.

Eric said, "Too cold. Let's play Nintendo."

"Too boring," Will and Scott said in unison.

"Let's dig out your Legos. I haven't played with Legos for years," Eric pushed his chair back and stood up.

"Nah, let's dig out your brother's stuff. Those guys that save the earth. You know." Will looked at Scott.

"Star Wars?"

"Make-believe guys. One's a skeleton." Will looked at Eric.

"Skeletor and . . . ." said Eric.

"Oh, yeah. She-ra, Cyclops, and . . . ." Scott looked at Will.

"Who cares," the boys said in unison.

"We'll make up the names. Just play," said Scott.

 1-56822-831-7

IDENTIFYING STORY ELEMENTS

1. Name the characters in the story.

   _____ _____ _____

2. What is the setting at the beginning of the story?
   ____ A. Scott's bedroom
   ____ B. Scott's living room
   ____ C. Scott's kitchen
   ____ D. Scott's basement

3. What is the problem in the story?
   ____ A. The boys can't think of anything to do.
   ____ B. The boys can't remember the names of the seven dwarfs.
   ____ C. The boys don't want to play Scrabble.
   ____ D. Will doesn't want to play anything anyone suggests.

4. How is the problem solved?

   _____

   _____

5. What is the main idea of the story? Check all that apply.
   ____ A. It is important to know the names of the seven dwarfs.

   ____ B. It is hard to decide what to play.

   ____ C. Playing together is more important than naming things.

   ____ D. Trivial Pursuit is a boring game.

ONE AFTERNOON IN MARCH

One afternoon in March, I found two silver dollars shining in a half melted snow bank. *Buried treasure* was my first thought. So I dug through the snow looking for more. Of course, I just ended up with really cold hands. I slipped the two coins into my pocket and went home colder but richer.

Two days later, Mary Ann and her little sister were searching the snow banks. *Finders keepers* was my first thought. I didn't need to get to the *losers weepers* part since Susy was already crying for real.

"I dropped them right here," she said between tears. Her hands were red from digging in the snow.

"Maybe they got shoved down the street with the snow plow. Let's dig over here." Mary Ann's voice sounded optimistic.

They'll never know was my second thought, and I walked past them toward Wisser's house.

"Phil, have you seen two silver dollars?" asked Mary Ann. Susy looked up from digging. Her eyes were hopeful.

"Coins?" *Look innocent* was my third thought.

"Yeah, Susy dropped two silver dollars along here last week."

"Silver dollars?"

"Yeah," said Susy. "They're thick and big." She brushed her red hands off on her jacket and wiped the tears from her face. Her eyes were as red as her hands.

Lie was my fourth thought. "As a matter of fact," I hesitated, "I dug two coins out of that snow bank just a few days ago. I wondered who might have lost them."

Susy leaped on me, hugging me. "Oh, thank you, thank you."

 1-56822-831-7

1. Name the characters in the story.

   _____   _____   _____

2. Who is narrating this story? _____

3. What is the setting? _____

4. What is the problem in the story?
   _____ A. Susy has lost two silver dollars in the snow.
   _____ B. Phil doesn't want to give up the coins he found.
   _____ C. Phil doesn't want to help Susy find her coins.
   _____ D. Mary Ann doesn't want to help her sister.

5. What do you think Phil thought when he hesitated at the end of the story?

   _____

   _____

6. What is the main idea of the story? Check all that apply.

   _____ A. "Finders keepers, losers weepers" is a stupid saying.

   _____ B. It is always better to be honest than rich.

   _____ C. It is easy to lie if you think you will get away with it.

   _____ D. "Finders keepers, losers weepers" is a good saying.

TROUBLE IS MY MIDDLE NAME

I'll admit, the list is long. I broke Mom's favorite blue vase playing baseball in the house. True, it was a home run, but that didn't cut much with Mom. I broke the back window. I didn't think I could break a window by shoving my hip against a door. Probably bad glass. I ruined the living room carpeting with the red spot the size of a basketball right in the middle of the entryway. I know the rules, no drinking in the living room, but I wasn't really drinking in there. I didn't even get a taste before I spilled the glass.

I guess "Trouble" is my middle name. At least that's what Mom says. So you won't be surprised when I tell you I'm in trouble once again. This time it really wasn't my fault.

I invited the guys over. Just a little game of baseball in the backyard. Joe was the one who wanted to put home plate so that any good batter would be hitting directly at Banters' house. I made them turn it so we were hitting into their garden. This time I was thinking.

Well, you can guess what happened. Joe hit a home-run ball that went deep. I chased it out of the park right into Banters' garden. Caught it too. I also destroyed three tomato plants and fell into the corn. It could have happened to anyone. It didn't have to be me, but remember my middle name. Trouble just haunts me.

Mrs. Banter wasn't so nice about the plants. She said I had to buy her some tomatoes in August to replace her harvest. She didn't say much about the corn, but she has plenty more corn plants.

These days, I play baseball only at the park. I'm working hard to find a different middle name.

 1-56822-831-7

1. Besides the narrator, name the important characters in the story.

   _____

2. What is the setting of the latest trouble caused by the narrator?

   _____

3. What is the problem in the story? Check all that apply.

   _____A. The narrator breaks and destroys things.

   _____B. Mrs. Banter was angry because her garden was damaged.

   _____C. Joe hit a home run.

   _____D. The narrator lied to Mrs. Banter.

4. How is the problem solved?

   _____

   _____

5. What is the main idea of the story? Check all that apply.

   _____A. If trouble is your middle name, there's not much you
           can do.

   _____B. If trouble is your middle name, you'd better be more
           careful.

   _____C. If trouble is your middle name, you can never change
           it.

   _____D. If trouble is your middle name, you better change it.

STEPHEN'S SECRET

Stephen Smith's birthday was the same day as his mother's. They were both born on March 15. Lots of people thought that was a bad luck birthday just because some ancient Roman king was killed that day. *The Ides of March,* people would say whenever he told them his birthday. Stephen wanted his birthday to be special for something good, not something bad.

Sometimes, he wished he could pick a birthday. He would pick a happy day like July 4. If his birthday were July 4, he would always have fireworks—brilliant reds, blues, and golds lighting up the sky. Plus, there would never be any school. He could invite his friends over for an all-day party. Everybody liked July 4. But when he really thought about it, even July 4 had drawbacks.

This year March and his birthday couldn't come soon enough. He was going to surprise his mother and change the Ides of March from bad luck to good luck. Keeping the birthday secret all winter was the hardest thing he had ever done. When he saw the first robin, he knew the secret would be popping out of the ground any day. He just wanted the green shoots to wait until March 15.

His mother always said, "Spring is my favorite time of year. The world turns green and you were born." This year Stephen wanted to make the world pop with beautiful colors, so he secretly planted fifty bulbs along his mother's flower garden.

As soon as March hit, he walked along the flower bed every day hoping to see tender green shoots. Finally, on March 1, a pair of leaves tipped in red pushed their way through the soil. By March 8, there were 15 more pairs of leaves. By March 15, Stephen's secret was two inches out of the soil. It was only a matter of time before he would have his own birthday fireworks—brilliant reds, blues, and golds popping open brightening the garden.

1. When was Stephen's birthday?_____

2. List two details that explain why he didn't like his birthday.

   _____

   _____

3. List two details that explain why he wanted his birthday on July 4.

   _____

   _____

4. How long did Stephen keep his secret? _____

5. What made Stephen invent his birthday fireworks?

   _____

   _____

   _____

YOU ARE A WINNER

Skip crossed only one set of fingers when he made a wish, avoided black cats, and never stepped on cracks when he walked on the sidewalk. He thought he was a perfect candidate to win something, anything. Skip did know that winning took more than crossing fingers and avoiding black cats and cracks.

Winning was the main reason Skip tried out for the track team. Skip wanted to hear the words, "You are the winner!" He imagined hearing his name read over the loud speaker. He wanted to be the center of attention for more than five minutes. He had never won anything in his entire life, unless you were counting games at someone's birthday party. However, Skip didn't work very hard at practice, and he didn't even make the team.

Skip spent his time kicking stones down the street. He pretended he was an NFL kicker in a championship game. The score was always 0-0, and his kick would cinch the title. He would drop the stone and boot it down the street. Then he would jump in the air cheering for himself. In one afternoon, he beat the Steelers, the Broncos, and the Chiefs.

Skip believed he would be a football star when he grew up. He thought, it doesn't really matter that I didn't make track. When I get to high school, I'll play football. Since I'm such a great kicker, I'll make that team easily. He imagined hearing his name read over the loud speaker. He might even keep playing in college, he thought. He really wanted to be a winner.

Drawing Conclusions

1. Who is the main character in the story? ____________________

2. Why does he want to be a winner?

____

____

3. What does he do that makes him believe he will be a football player?

____

4. Has he ever won anything?

____

____

5. Will he ever become a winner? Circle one: Yes No Explain your answer.

____

____

____

____

____

____

FREE KITTENS

"Free Kittens," the sign read. I've always wanted a kitten, Marcy thought, plus this one is free. *Walk away,* Marcy could hear her mom's voice in her head, *Don't even look. Just walk away.* She read the sign again and thought, Maybe I can say I found it. I could put up signs around the neighborhood advertising a lost kitten. When no one claimed it, mom would break down.

Marcy read the sign one more time. Just a peek, she thought and walked over to look inside the box. Two kittens, one black and one white, were curled in the corner. Marcy picked up the white one. It had the pinkest nose and a black ring around its left eye. The kitten purred in Marcy's hand.

"They're a pair," said the little girl behind the box. "The other one has a white circle around its left eye."

"Salt and pepper," Marcy said, and the little girl laughed.

"You can take them both," the girl said. "They've never been apart."

"Both?" Marcy picked up the second kitten. She held them next to each other. They were, indeed, a pair. She nestled the kittens under her chin and listened to them purr.

Marcy could hear her mother's voice, *Walk away. Just walk away.* She thought, Mom will never believe two lost kittens.

"They like you," the girl said.

"Yeah, listen to them purr." Marcy rubbed Pepper against her chin.

"The mother died," the girl said. "She was hit by a car."

"Hit by a car?" Marcy said. She thought, Mom couldn't turn away two kittens without a mother. She put the kittens back in the box. She read the sign again and said, "I'll take 'em."

1. How many times does Marcy read the sign, "Free Kittens"? ____

2. What words of advice would Marcy's mom say if she were with Marcy?

_____

3. What is the first story Marcy plans to tell her mother so she can take a kitten home?

_____

_____

4. What convinces Marcy to take both kittens?

_____

_____

_____

5. Write the story Marcy will tell her mother to convince her to keep the two kittens.

_____

_____

_____

How Can You Believe That?

"Hot!" shouted Marla as she leaped out of her chair and to the refrigerator. She opened the freezer and pulled out an ice cube.

"I wouldn't do that if I were you. That ice'll stick to your tongue," said Kenshee.

"Who told you that?" Marla stuck out her tongue and pressed the cube flat against it.

"My grandma."

Marla garbled, "How can a melting ice cube stick to my tongue?"

"OK! Don't believe me."

Marla dropped the melted cube into the sink and returned to the table. The ice did not pull the skin off her tongue. "See. It worked, but I just killed some taste buds, you know."

"How?" Kenshee asked.

"When you burn your tongue, you lose taste buds," Marla repeated. "You start with 9,000 taste buds as a baby, and each time you burn your tongue, some die."

"Who told you that?"

"Phil. He said his uncle told him. And his uncle works at a hospital."

"Phil's uncle is a security guard. You can't believe him."

"It's true. I probably lost 20 buds just now."

"Hopefully not the ones for chocolate."

"His uncle says all 9,000 are on the surface of the tongue. They are raised in groups of about 100." Marla blew on her hot chocolate. "You don't have to be a doctor to know facts."

"True, but 9,000 taste buds? I can't believe that," said Kenshee.

1. Is Kenshee's warning about ice correct? Circle one: Yes No

2. What makes Marla's statement about taste buds hard to believe?

    _____

    _____

3. Why doesn't Kenshee believe Phil's uncle is correct?

    _____

4. What is the purpose of this story? Check one.

    _____ A. To illustrate only doctors can know facts about the
    body.

    _____ B. To illustrate anyone can know facts about the body.

    _____ C. To illustrate a person should always doubt the beliefs
    of others.

    _____ D. To illustrate sometimes a person should never doubt
    the beliefs of others.

5. Do you believe Marla? Circle one: Yes No Explain your answer.

    _____

    _____

    _____

IT'S NOT MY FAULT!

"You be the judge. I need an objective opinion. Tracy says I'm a liar." I took a bite of my ham sandwich.

"About what?" Heather said.

"It doesn't matter. I'm honest, right?"

"Honest about what?" Heather took a sip of milk.

"Honest. You know, trustworthy, direct, truthful." I smiled.

Heather hesitated, then nodded. "Yeah, you're pretty honest. Except the time you lied to your folks about your math grade. And then the time you. . . . "

"Math grades don't count, and the time I went shopping with Tracy doesn't count either."

"Shopping? What about the time you went shopping with Tracy?"

"It's not my fault that Tracy didn't want you to come. I didn't want to hurt your feelings. So she told me to tell you I was sick."

"So you lied to me." Heather raised her voice.

"I didn't lie. Tracy made up the lie."

"Don't blame Tracy because you lied to me." Heather ripped the cellophane covering off her brownie.

"It's not my fault. Plus, you're way too sensitive." I gulped my milk.

"Cheryl, the point is simple. You lie to your friends and then blame them for your mistakes." Heather took a bite of her brownie. "So, no, you're not really honest."

"Forget it." I shoved the last of my sandwich into my mouth. I could see that Heather was still hurt about Tracy. She wouldn't understand my problem. "I gotta go. I'll see you tomorrow."

1-56822-831-7

1. Put the correct name next to the detail to clarify the story.

Heather   Tracy   Cheryl

_____A. Went shopping with Tracy.

_____B. Told Heather she was sick.

_____C. Blamed Tracy for her problems.

2. Why does Heather get angry? _____

3. What do you think was the real reason Cheryl asked Heather to be the judge? Check one.

_____A. She wanted advice.

_____B. She wanted an objective opinion.

_____C. She wanted Heather to side with her against Tracy.

_____D. She wanted an honest opinion.

4. Why does Cheryl say "Forget it." and leave? Check one.

_____ A. She didn't get the answer she wanted.

_____ B. She was hurt by Heather's unfairness.

_____ C. She felt bad that she'd hurt Heather's feelings.

_____ D. She was wrong, and she knew it.

5. Does Cheryl really want an objective opinion? Circle one: Yes No

SLEEPWALKING

Dad settles on the couch. I stand tall, grasp my note cards, and smile. "Be honest. I need a good grade," I say. He nods and I begin. "Ever fight  falling asleep for seven hours straight? Ever want control over your life?" I pause for effect. "If you answered yes, then you have something in common with me and all students."

"Nice opening," Dad says, and I smile.

"Students all over the United States are plagued with sleep deprivation. If schools really wanted students to learn better, they would begin school at 11:00 and end school at 2:00."

"That's a bit exaggerated," Dad says.

I nod, stand up straight, glance quickly at my note cards and begin again. "Research shows the pre-teen brain needs 10-12 hours of sleep. Research suggests that children learn best after 10:00. Studies also indicate attention spans are only 20 minutes long."

"Is that true?" Dad asks. "Sounds like you're twisting facts."

"Sort of," I say. I shuffle my cards and continue. "The trouble is 7:30 is when school starts, which means most students are really sleepwalking. Nobody wakes up until lunch time. Plus, if the attention span is only 20 minutes, it makes sense to change classes to 20 minutes each. Students would be more alert and would learn more. Therefore, I recommend a later start time and 20-minute classes." I smile.

"I recommend you rethink the point of the speech."

"But what about my delivery?"

"Good voice and delivery, but your speech is not logical."

"I'm getting graded on speech skills and facts, not logic, Dad."

"Winona, rethink the speech." Dad uses his better-do-what-I-say voice. I shuffle my note cards and think, *maybe he's right. I could add the facts about brain waves and learning to read, or a list of the eight intelligences.* I smile. "Ok, I'll add more facts."

1. When a story is told in first person, a narrator tells a personal story from his or her point of view. Who is the narrator of this story?

   _____

2. What does Dad say makes Winona's speech good? Check one.

   _____ A. It has good facts.

   _____ B. It has a good opening.

   _____ C. It has a good idea.

   _____ D. She has good delivery.

3. What does Dad say makes Winona's speech weak? Check one.

   _____ A. It twists facts and information.

   _____ B. It has a weak conclusion.

   _____ C. It is not logical.

   _____ D. She uses a weak voice.

4. What does Dad suggest to improve Winona's speech?

   _____

5. First-person point of view allows the reader to see the thoughts of the narrator. Will Winona fix her speech and make it better? Circle one: Yes   No   Explain your answer by reviewing Winona's thoughts.

   _____

   _____

FINDING MY KEYS

Ok, where did I leave them this time? I flatten my palm as if I am holding my house keys. I think aloud, "I just had them in my hand." Then I mumble almost inaudibly. "When I came home last night, I put my purse and keys on the kitchen counter. Mom yelled to clean up the counter. I cleaned the counter, I took my purse to my bedroom, but the keys weren't there." I retrace my steps from the kitchen to my bedroom. No keys on the counter and no keys on my bed, the floor, my dresser, or my bookcase.

I say aloud, "Wait, I didn't use them to open the door. Kimmy was home already, and the door was open. I never took them out of my purse. So they're in my purse." I rummage through my purse, no keys. I think maybe I left them at school. But I reject that thought immediately.

I sit on my bed, lean against the pillow, and shut my eyes. "Yesterday. What did I do with the keys yesterday?" I say aloud. Then I roll the memory tapes. I'm wearing my red sweater. I have the keys in my hand. I unlock the door because Kimmy forgot her keys. We set our junk on the counter, and like always, Mom yelled, "Susy! Kimmy! Put your things away." Kimmy picked up her stuff, but I didn't. When I came home from Sarah's, my stuff was on my bedroom floor, and Mom was mad. I apologized, did my homework, and packed my backpack.

The memory stops, and I shout, "No keys." So they are in my room. I pick up all the clothes thrown in the corner, look under the bed, pick up the books and papers next to my bed and drop them back in place. No keys.

"OK! OK!" I say aloud. "They have to be here." I sit back on my bed, lean against the pillows, and shut my eyes. Yesterday. What did I do with the keys yesterday? I think.

   1-56822-831-7

1. Number the events of the story in their correct order.

_____ Susy loses her keys.

_____ Susy opens the door because Kimmy forgot her keys.

_____ Susy puts her keys on the kitchen counter.

_____ Susy packs her backpack for school.

_____ Kimmy cleans her stuff off the counter.

2. Where do you think Susy's keys are? Check one.

_____ A. In her backpack.

_____ B. In her bedroom

_____ C. Kimmy has them.

_____ D. Mother has them.

3. Why does Susy lose her keys so often?

_____ A. Her sister is always taking her things.

_____ B. Her mother moves things around all the time.

_____ C. She never puts things away.

_____ D. She is forgetful.

4. Make a prediction: Will Susy find her keys? Circle one: Yes No
   Explain your answer.

_____

WHO SHOULD WIN?

Mrs. Ponter always had a difficult time selecting an English award winner. She really disliked giving recognition to just one student. Many years she wanted to give out six or seven awards. This year it was easier because there were just two very deserving candidates, but that also made the decision even harder.

How could she choose between Alexander Curry and Margarete Chico? Both students received straight "A's." Both students always did their homework. Both students had a 98% average on their spelling and vocabulary tests, and both students tied for first place in the PTSA writing contest.

Margarete was the best student in her second-hour class. She always raised her hand, tutored other students, and was a real leader in group work. Margarete helped edit the yearbook, and she took almost all of the pictures for it as well. The yearbook company gave Margarete an award for her creativity. However, Margarete did mess around in class. Just last week, Mrs. Ponter had to tell her three times to pay attention.

On the other hand, Alexander was the best student in her third-hour class. He was shy and quiet, but he was the top speller in all of sixth grade and had perfect attendance. He wrote the best stories and was the editor of the school paper. Alexander was quite a reader. He probably read 40 books just this year. He always had a book in his hands. As a matter of fact, sometimes he read during class. Just last week, Mrs. Ponter had to tell him three times to pay attention.

As Mrs. Ponter considered the students, she found it harder and harder to decide which one was best. Finally, she discovered one thing that set the two students apart, and decided to give the award to Alexander.

1. Fill in the Venn diagram below to determine what caused Mrs. Ponter to select Alexander for the English Award.

Margarete   Margarete & Alexander   Alexander

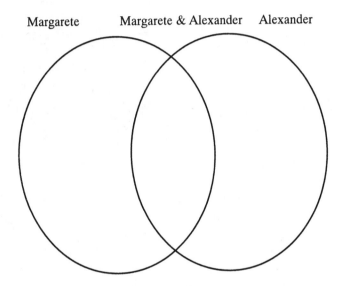

2. Why did Mrs. Ponter select Alexander?

_____

_____

3. Do you agree with her choice? Circle one: Yes   No   Explain your answer.

_____

_____

HOW COULD THIS HAPPEN TO ME?

The ophthalmologist said, "Sammy's headaches are caused from eye strain. He needs to rest his eyes. No reading for awhile. No television, either."

Sammy's mother said, "Sammy? Eye strain? Sammy never reads, and we already limit his television."

Sammy sat quietly. He didn't want to admit the truth. The truth was he played too much solitaire.

Sammy was the solitaire champion. True, he never really competed with anyone because he played on his computer at home, but he felt like a champion just the same. His high score was 5,400 points.

Sammy rushed home from school every day to play solitaire. He could play 30 or 40 games before his mother arrived home from work.

He played so often that he could count the cards, and he could guess which cards were still face down. He almost always knew which pile hid the card he really needed.

Sammy sat as the doctor gave his mother instructions. His mother nodded and agreed. Sammy shook his head in wonder. "How could this happen to me?" he said. He nodded and agreed that he would give up reading and television. He would rest his eyes for a week and return to be checked again.

The next day when Sammy arrived home from school and flipped the computer switch on, he was surprised to find a password installed in the system. A small note attached to the corner of the monitor read, "Sammy, go outside, and play. Love, Mom."

68 1-56822-831-7

1. Why did Sammy's mother take him to the doctor?

_____

2. Why was Sammy's mother confused about the doctor's diagnosis? Check all that apply.

_____ A. Sammy already wore glasses.

_____ B. Sammy never read.

_____ C. Sammy played outside all the time.

_____ D. Sammy rarely watched television.

3. What information did Sammy keep from the doctor and his mother?

_____

4. Would Sammy's secret cause eye strain? Circle one: Yes   No
   Use facts from the reading to support your thinking.

_____

_____

5. Why did Sammy say, "How could this happen to me?" _____

_____ A. He was confused about the doctor's diagnosis too.

_____ B. He didn't understand the problem.

_____ C. He didn't want to admit to playing solitaire so
   much.

_____ D. He was sad that he wouldn't be able to read.

6. Why did Sammy's mother install a password on the computer?

SOLLIE, THE ROCK

Water skiing is like flying. If you aren't afraid of getting up, you'll enjoy the ride. That's what I told my best friend, Sollie, before we spent the afternoon trying to get him up on skis for the first time.

I thought it would be easy. Sollie is a seal, sleek and smooth in the water, bobbing in and out of the waves. I thought someone so agile would find skiing easy. It didn't dawn on me until the fourth try that Sollie is shaped more like a rock than a bird.

On his first try, Sollie let go of the tow rope when Dad hit the gas. He sank as fast as the *Titanic*. The only things visible were the tips of his skis.

On his second try, Sollie leaned into the skis, flipping head over heels like a gymnast falling off the balance beam. His skis formed an "X" that marked the spot where he disappeared.

On the third try, Sollie stood up, teetered forward then back as if he were a rag doll. His biggest mistake was holding on to the rope after he lost both skis. He flopped about behind the boat like a giant carp until he finally let go.

On the fourth try, Sollie bent his knees, straightened his back, and flew around the lake behind the boat as if he were a professional skier. He jumped the wake, rolled out next to the boat, and waved at me. He was "the man." After three times around the lake, Sollie let go of the rope. He returned to his former self and dropped into the water like a rock.

70   1-56822-831-7

1. Identify the following lines from the story as metaphors or similes.

Metaphor: a direct comparison between two unlike things. Example: Bobby is a mouse.

Simile: an indirect comparison between two unlike things using the words *like, as,* or *as if* to make the comparison. Example: Bobby is like a mouse.

_____ A. Sollie is a seal, sleek and smooth in the water, bobbing in and out of the waves.

_____ B. Sollie is shaped more like a rock than a bird.

_____ C. He sank as fast as the *Titanic*.

_____ D. He flopped about behind the boat like a giant carp until he finally let go.

2. What do the similes above suggest about Sollie?

_____

_____

3. Why is this sentence not a simile or metaphor? _____
Sollie bent his knees, straightened his back, and flew around the lake behind the boat as if he were a professional skier.

_____ A. It does not make a comparison.

_____ B. It makes a comparison between like things.

_____ C. It makes a contrast rather than a comparison.

_____ D. The comparison is not between a person and an animal.

I Never Thought of That

"For homework, do the even problems on page 158 and 159."

I dropped my mouth open, looked at Mrs. Bronswell with a blank stare, then tucked my head into my arms and started to cry. When the bell rang, the class rushed out the door. I waited, hoping to slip out unnoticed.

"You are too good of a student to sleep in class," said Mrs. Bronswell.

"I wasn't," I mustered, trying not to sound like I'd been crying.

"You have a cold?"

"No," I stumbled, "I mean, I'm not feeling well."

"What's wrong?" she asked.

I burst out into tears. It was as if I had just gone head over heels over my bike handles, flying through the air, face first, toward the cement.

"What's wrong?" Mrs. Bronswell sounded worried now.

"I . . . I. . . . I" I couldn't get any words out.

"Sit down, Alex, and just cry. We'll talk in a minute."

She handed me a big clump of tissues, and I cried. Finally, I said, "It's the last straw. Math homework. This weekend I have a presentation to the flower and garden luncheon and a trumpet solo at church. I have to help my grandpa with his lawn work, and I volunteered to rake the nature trails at the park. Then I have 200 pages of English to read and a log to write— I sort of left it to the last minute—a city to build for history class, that's about halfway done, a science experiment to write up, a report to write for health, and now two pages of math. I'll never get it all done."

"Whoa," she said, "I'd cry too."

"I . . . I . . . I" I blew my nose and wiped my tears.

"Let's make a list. Things that have to be done, and things that are low priorities. Then, do the difficult task of choosing what not to do," she said.

"You mean, don't do my math, if I don't have time?"

"That's right. You might get a bad grade, but you can't do everything. If you can't get it all done, you have to make choices."

I took a huge breath as if a 1,000-pound weight was lifted off my shoulder. "Choices," I said. "Wow. I never thought of that."

"More important, Alex. Try to avoid getting overloaded in the future."

1. Why did Alex cry? Check one.

    _____ A. He hated math homework.

    _____ B. He didn't know how to do the homework.

    _____ C. He had too much to do.

    _____ D. He was afraid he would get a bad grade.

2. Using your best judgment, insert the tasks Alex must finish this weekend into the two lists below.

Things that have to be done	Things that might be done

3. What good advice did Mrs. Bronswell give Alex that he could use for the rest of his life? Check all that apply.

    _____ A. Make a list of your activities.

    _____ B. Avoid overloading yourself with activities and commitments.

    _____ C. Don't do your math and take a bad grade.

    _____ D. Make choices and accept the consequences.

ANSWER KEY

The Sad Story of Seven Birds   Page 3
1. Sad Story
2. Hunters Destroy
   Settlers Destroy
3. Man would be the culprit
   Being prey to hunters
   Being victim of disappearing
   nesting grounds and habitats
4. C
5. Answers may vary.
6. Answers may vary.

From Slave to Inventor   Page 5
1. A. worked hard
   B. agricultural experiments
   C. reason, returned, help, farmers
   D. turned, peanut, major, cash,
       crop
2. C
3. Answers may vary.
4. Answers may vary.

Milk: Not For Everybody   Page 7
1. Answers may vary. Some details
   are: Milk contains calcium, vitamins
   A, C, and D; many people can drink
   milk; babies live on it; ice cream
   and cheese are made from milk.
2. Enzyme, lactose intolerance,
   lactase, genes, digest, intestinal,
   produce.
3. Answers may vary.
4. Answers may vary. However, the
   answer should indicate that milk is
   not healthy for all people.

Man's Super-structure   Page 9
1. Bones are a living organ, serve as
   the support for muscles and organs,
   give the body size and shape,
   contain nerves and blood vessels,
   grow and are continually being
   replaced.
2. Nourishment, osteoclasts,
   osteoblasts, cells, platelets.

3. Answers may vary.
4. Answers may vary. However,
   answers should state that bones are
   an important living organ.

Violent Crime Declining   Page 11
1. Homicide, rape, robbery, and
   aggravated assault.
2. Reports to police or FBI and
   surveys
3. Total violent crime, crimes
   recorded by police and FBI,
   victimizations reported to police,
   arrests for violent crimes.
4. 328,413
5. Increased
6. Answers may vary.

Ancient Surgery   Page 13
1. The holes were carefully scraped.
   The bone had begun to grow back,
   indicating a healing period. The
   holes did not cause the person's
   death.
2. Pressure on the brain, headaches,
   epilepsy, or mental illness.
3. They interviewed tribes in Africa
   that also used this procedure.
4. The surgery was too effective and
   suggested it had been used for
   years to achieve that high level of
   effectiveness.

Early Writing Is Still Writing   Page 15
1. Answers may vary, but these are
   possible notes. Misconceptions:
   scribbling is not writing, practicing
   letters is important, dictation was a
   good writing activity.
   Discoveries: scribbling is writing,
   children should write even if they
   do not know their alphabet, children
   should read their scribbling as if it
   is writing.

2. They become better readers.
3. Answers may vary.

Cross-Country or Downhill? Page 17
1. Cross-country
no ski lifts, no tall hills, can go out your back door, can ski on flat land, races last 50-120 minutes, races are 9-30 miles long, skis are short and narrow, boots fit below the ankle and are attached at the toe only
Both cross-country and downhill use poles, need snow, racers try for speed, require special skis and boots
Downhill Skiing
need tall hills, usually ski at resorts, need ski lifts, races are short usually the length of the hill or less, go down the hill at speeds of 80 mph, use long narrow skis, boots protect the ankle and go above it, boots are attached at toe and heel.
2. Answers may vary.
3. Answers may vary.

I Need My Eight Hours   Page 19
1. 4
2. 1½ hours
3. During REM sleep
4. 8 hours
5. 16 hours
6. Answers will vary.
7. Answers will vary.
8. Graphs will vary.

Making Old-Fashioned Fudge
Page 21
1. Smooth consistency and taste
2. Patience and tools
3. 1. Prepare cold water in sauce pan.
   2. Combine ingredients and stir
   3. Boil, waiting for soft-ball stage.
   4. Remove from heat, add butter and vanilla and beat.
4. Use a microwave.
5. #1, 3, and 4

Icebiking: Challenge, Insanity, or Fun?
Page 23
1. Answers may vary.
2. Recreation, commuting, camping trips
3. cold and snow
4. Don't put your bike away when winter arrives
5. studded tires, warm clothing, boots, and helmet
6. Answers will vary.

How Cold Is It Really?   Page 25
1. 32°F
2. 10°F
3. Wind
4. A. -5°F
   B. -5°F
   C. -3°F
   D. -10°F
5. D

Replaced But Not Forgotten   Page 27
1. Old Lighthouses used fires, staffed by lighthouse keepers, saved shipwrecked sailors, captains depended on charts
Both old and new lighthouses warn of danger
Are on day and night
New Lighthouses use electric lights like airports, staffed by U.S. Coast Guard, captains use radar
2. Answers will vary.
3. Answers will vary. Most students should suggest that there are fewer wrecks due to improved shipping technology.

From Poor Farm Boy to President
Page 29
1. Shopkeeper, clerk, postmaster, rail splitter, congressman, and lawyer.
2. Honest, motivated, and dedicated
3. No
4. #1: in 1860
   #2: as a statesman

#3: as a child
#4: before studying law
#5: as president
5. 3, 4, 1, 2, 5

Before Television, There Was Radio
Page 31
1. Lone Ranger, Shadow, Green Hornet
2. Jack Benny, Red Skelton, George Burns
3. Entertain people, give news, and part of daily life
4. Radio. Radio took only ten years to become widely popular.
5. He was a Texas Ranger, had a faithful Indian friend named Tonto, rode a white horse named Silver, wore a black mask, hid his identity, wore a white hat, and yelled "Hi-O Silver."

From Dreams to Reality **Page 33**
1. Answers may vary.
2. Yes, 1903, 1961, 1963, 1965, 1968, 1969, 1969, 1972, 1986
3. Manned   Unmanned
   1903 Orville and 1968 - first
   Wilbur Wright   orbit of
                     moon
   1961 first manned space flight
   1963 first woman cosmonaut
   1965 first space walk
   1969 first man on moon
   1969 moon exploration
   1986 *Mir* space station

Planning a Budget and Sticking to It
Page 35
1. Expenditures: What you spend your money on.
   Debit: Items you subtract from your income.
   Credit: Items you add to your income
   Cash Flow: The relationship between your debits and credits. The amount of money you spend.

2. 1. Look at your expenditures
   2. Determine debits and credits
   3. Determine cash flow and savings goals
3. Answers may vary.

I Just Talk on It **Page 37**
1. A. Project a picture
   B. From an antenna to a satellite
2. Cables, optical fibers, satellites, and radio transmissions.
3. Answers may vary.

Sending Love Through Cyberspace
Page 39
1. *Love* and *Cyberspace*
2. *Cyberspace* is the name for transferring information on the Internet.
3. Internet, Web site, computer applications, e-mail.
4. Alex e-mailed Sese a valentine.
5. B
6. Sese smiled and wrote Alex notes, and she laughed at his jokes.

The Lesson **Page 41**
1. Leah
2. Leah feels she is wrong and does not want the listener to believe she is defending her actions.
3. Leah received a "C" on her last test and was grounded.
4. She had a premonition when she missed the bus and was late to school.
5. A

By Saturday Noon **Page 43**
1. Saturday noon was the deadline to have her room clean.
2. Margaret is a neat-freak.
3. Margaret is too clean. Mother wouldn't let her throw her clothes down the laundry chute. Chelsea got sick and couldn't help her. Jen

decided to leave early to go shopping.
4. Answers will vary.

To the Moon Page 45
1. It means to hit a ball out of the park.
2. Both boys like to hit the ball hard, and they strike out often. Plus, both boys never bunt.
3. The boys always try to hit the ball hard and put it out of the park by hitting it to the moon.
4. Steve suggests that the boys have the same problem hitting the ball too hard. Plus the coach says, "Steve, nothin' fancy."
5. D

Can You Name the Seven Dwarfs? Page 47
1. Scott, Eric, Will
2. C
3. A
4. The boys make up the names of the characters and just have fun playing.
5. C

One Afternoon in March Page 49
1. Mary Ann, Susy, Phil
2. Phil
3. A street
4. B
5. Answers may vary. He decided to be honest and tell the truth.
6. A and B

Trouble Is My Middle Name Page 51
1. Mom, Joe, Mrs. Banter
2. The narrator's backyard.
3. A and B
4. She plays baseball at the park and is more careful. She also repairs Mrs. Banter's garden and apologizes.
5. B and D

Stephen's Secret Page 53
1. March 15
2. It is the same day as his mother's. It is the same day a Roman king was killed.
3. It has fireworks and there is no school so he can have an all-day party.
4. All winter.
5. He wanted to surprise his mother and change the Ides of March from bad luck to good luck.

You Are a Winner Page 55
1. Skip
2. Skip wants to be the center of attention.
3. He kicks rocks down the street and pretends he is making great plays.
4. No
5. No. Answers may vary.

Free Kittens Page 57
1. Four
2. Walk away. Don't even look. Just walk away.
3. She found the kitten.
4. They are a matching pair.
5. Answers may vary, but the fact that the mother was killed must be part of the story.

How Can You Believe That? Page 59
1. No
2. Answers may vary. Possibly the large number of taste buds.
3. He is only a security guard.
4. B
5. Answers may vary.

It's Not My Fault! Page 61
1. A. Cheryl
   B. Cheryl
   C. Cheryl
2. She discovers Cheryl lied to her.

   1-56822-831-7

3. C
4. A
5. No

Sleepwalking   **Page 63**
1. Winona
2. B
3. C
4. Rethink her speech.
5. No. She says she will add facts. Facts will not make the speech more logical.

Finding My Keys   **Page 65**
1. 5, 1, 2, 3, 4
2. C
3. C
4. Answers may vary.

Who Should Win?   **Page 67**
1. Margarete
   raises her hand
   tutors others
   edits the yearbook
   takes pictures
   won a creativity award

   Both Margarete and Alexander
   do their homework
   are the best student in their hour
   are tied for the PTSA writing award
   do not pay attention

   Alexander
   top speller in sixth grade
   perfect attendance
   edits the newspaper
   reads 40 books independently
2. Answers may vary.
3. Answers may vary.

How Could This Happen to Me?
                                    Page 69
1. Sammy had headaches.
2. B and D
3. He played solitaire on the computer every day.
4. Yes. Sammy played 30-40 games of solitaire every day.
5. C
6. The password kept Sammy off the computer.

Sollie, the Rock   **Page 71**
1. A. metaphor
   B. simile
   C. simile
   D. simile
2. Sollie is not a very good swimmer.
3. B

I Never Thought of That   **Page 73**
1. C
2. Answers may vary. However, these things should be on the "have to be done" side: presentation to the Flower and Garden Lunch and rake nature trails—both of these are commitments to other people and the consequences effect more than the person making the choices.
3. A, B, and D